ACCOUNTING

A book for beginners to learn Financial Accounting Basics

GW00399967

Tilly Maureens

Accounting

DEDICATION

This research paper is dedicated to my dear father, who has been nicely my supporter until my research was fully finished, and my beloved mother who, for months past, has encouraged me attentively with her fullest and truest attention to accomplish my work with truthful self-confidence.

TABLE-OF-CONTENTS

Tilly Maureens

Accounting

Financial Accounting Basics

The field of accounting is often thought of as a set of complex business rules and endless numbers. Well in short, it is. I say that only jokingly, though. Accounting, at its heart, is actually a set of very simple concepts and principles. Once you understand the basics of accounting, you will be able to grasp just about any business or accounting concept. I see it only fitting that we start our accounting training at the beginning with the purpose of financial accounting.

This accounting book explains the fundamentals of accounting like identifying business activities, recording transactions, and understanding the double entry accounting system. I walk you through the basics of accounts, journals, and ledgers as well as the financial statement elements. Essentially, the basics section will give you an understanding of the general accounting terms that are the building blocks of your accounting knowledge.

Here are the basic topics of financial accounting. I wrote an explanation of each concept along with easy to follow examples.

Financial Accounting

o What is Financial Accounting?

Accounting in general deals with identifying business activities, like sales to customers, recording these activities, like journalizing, and communicating these activities with people outside the organization with financial statements.

Financial accounting, however, is a subsection of the general field of accounting that focuses on gathering and compiling data in order to present it to external users in a usable form. So what does that mean? Basically, financial accounting's main purpose is to provide useful, financial information to people or groups outside of companies often called external users.

o Who Uses Financial Accounting?

Unlike company management or internal users, external users of financial information are not directly involved in running the business or organization. They are outsiders to the business and only have limited information about companies' operations, financial position, and well being. In other words, external users need financial information about companies in order to support their financial decisions.

The ultimate goal of financial accounting is to compile business transactions and other input documents like invoices and sales receipts in the form of general purpose financial statements that can be understood by external users.

The key concept here is that external users must be able to understand and use this financial information when they are making decisions about the company. If the information can't be used, it is worthless. That is why the FASB has created a series of accounting principles and concepts to make sure financial statements are comparable and understandable.

o **Different Types of Financial Statement Users**

There are many different types of external users who want or need financial information for different purposes. All of these external users have something in common. They are interested in doing business with a company but only have limited access to the company's financial information. Financial accounting aims as providing financial information that is reliable, relevant, and comparable to these external users.

Here is a list of the most common external users of financial information and how they use it.

o **Shareholders or Investors**

Shareholders and other investors are usually the first group of external users that comes to mind. Investors in general want to assess the value of a company in order to decide whether it is worth buying, selling, or holding their stock. Investors read financial statements to help predict future performance and company worth.

o **Lenders or Creditors**

Lenders or creditors also use financial statements to base the decisions on because they want to know if a company is creditworthy enough to pay off its current loans or borrow additional funds. Creditors study financial statements in order to analyse the liquidity and sustainability of a company.

o **Customers**

It might sound unlikely, but many customers study financial statements before making major purchases. For instance, large companies will study financial statements of their potential suppliers in order to make sure they are fiscally sound. A company, benefits from long-term relationships with its suppliers. It wants to make sure of potential suppliers' longevity before it goes into business with them.

o **Suppliers**

Suppliers also use the financial statements of customers to judge whether they are creditworthy enough to extend credit. For example, if a customer orders 100,000 units from a supplier, the supplier wants to know whether the customer will be able to pay for these units before the supplies incurs the expense of producing them.

o **Unions**

Unions use financial information to judge whether employee wage rates and benefit packages are fair. They also use this information to assess future job prospects and bargain for higher wages and better benefits.

o **Brokers and Analysts**

Brokers and analysts are often potential investors that use financial information about companies to chart performance trends and growth rates. These external users create reports that influence current investor's opinions and actions.

o **Press**

Finally, the last main external user is the press. Although the press does not use financial information for its decision bases, it does report on the financial information of companies. Networks are multi-million dollar businesses that simply report financial information about other companies.

As you can see, the list of external users is almost endless. Financial accounting aims to provide all of these groups with information that can be useful for them in their individual decision making processes.

Accounting Equation

o **What is the Accounting Equation?**

The accounting equation, also called the basic accounting equation, forms the foundation for all accounting systems. In fact, the entire double entry accounting concept is based on the basic accounting equation. This simple equation illustrates two facts about a company: what it owns and what it owes.

The accounting equation equates a company's assets to its liabilities and equity. This shows all company assets are acquired by either debt or equity financing. For example, when a company is started, its assets are first purchased with either cash the company received from loans or cash the company received from investors. Thus, all of the company's assets stem from either creditors or investors i.e. liabilities and equity.

o **Basic Accounting Equation Formula**

Here is the basic accounting equation.

Accounting Equation				
Assets	=	Liabilities	+	Equity

As you can see, assets equal the sum of liabilities and owner's equity. This makes sense when you think about it because liabilities and equity are essentially just sources of funding for companies to purchase assets.

The equation is generally written with liabilities appearing before owner's equity because creditors usually have to be repaid before investors in a bankruptcy. In this sense, the liabilities are considered more current than the equity. This is consistent with financial reporting where current assets and liabilities are always reported before long-term assets and liabilities.

This equation holds true for all business activities and transactions. Assets will always equal liabilities and owner's equity. If assets increase, either liabilities or owner's equity must increase to balance out the equation. The opposite is true if liabilities or equity increase.

Now that we have a basic understanding of the equation, let's take a look at each accounting equation component starting with the assets.

o **Accounting Equation Components**

Assets

An asset is a resource that is owned or controlled by the company to be used for future benefits. Some assets are tangible like cash while others are theoretical or intangible like goodwill or copyrights.

Another common asset is a receivable. This is a promise to be paid from another party. Receivables arise when a company provides a service or sells a product to someone on credit.

All of these assets are resources that a company can use for future benefits. Here are some common examples of assets:

1. Current Assets

    - Cash

    - Accounts Receivable

    - Prepaid Expense

2. Fixed Assets

    - Vehicle

    - Buildings

3. Intangible Assets

    - Goodwill

    - Copyrights

    - Patents

Liabilities

A liability, in its simplest terms, is an amount of money owed to another person or organization. Said a different way, liabilities are creditors' claims on company assets because this is the amount of assets creditors would own if the company liquidated.

A common form of liability is a payable. Payables are the opposite of receivables. When a company purchases goods or services from other companies on credit, a payable is recorded to show that the company promises to pay the other companies for their assets.

Here are some examples of some of the most common liabilities:

- Accounts payable
- Bank loans
- Lines of Credit
- Personal Loans
- Officer Loans
- Unearned income

Equity

Equity represents the portion of company assets that shareholders or partners own. In other words, the shareholders or partners own the remainder of assets once all of the liabilities are paid off.

Owners can increase their ownership share by contributing money to the company or decrease equity by withdrawing company funds. Likewise, revenues increase equity while expenses decrease equity.

Here are some common equity accounts:

- Owner's Capital
- Owner's Withdrawals
- Officer Loans
- Unearned income
- Common stock
- Paid-In Capital

o **Example**

How to use the Accounting Equation

Let's take a look at the formation of a company to illustrate how the accounting equation works in a business situation.

Suellen is an entrepreneur who wants to start a company selling speakers for car stereo systems. After saving up money for a year, Jack decides it is time to officially start his business. He forms Speakers, Inc. and contributes $100,000 to the company in exchange for all of its newly issued shares. This business transaction increases company cash and increases equity by the same amount.

Accounting Equation		
$100,000		$100,000
⬆		⬆
Assets	= Liabilities	+ Equity

After the company formation, Speakers, Inc. needs to buy some equipment for installing speakers, so it purchases $20,000 of installation equipment from a manufacturer for cash. In this case, Speakers, Inc. uses its cash to buy another asset, so the asset account is decreased from the disbursement of cash and increased by the addition of installation equipment.

Accounting Equation		
$20,000 $20,000		
⬇ ⬆		
Assets	= Liabilities	+ Equity

Accounting

After six months, Speakers, Inc. is growing rapidly and needs to find a new place of business. Suellen decides it makes the most financial sense for Speakers, Inc. to buy a building. Since Speakers, Inc. doesn't have $500,000 in cash to pay for a building, it must take out a loan. Speakers, Inc. purchases a $500,000 building by paying $100,000 in cash and taking out a $400,000 mortgage. This business transaction decreases assets by the $100,000 of cash disbursed, increases assets by the new $500,000 building, and increases liabilities by the new $400,000 mortgage.

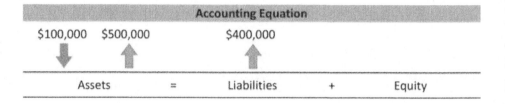

As you can see, all of these transactions always balance out the accounting equation. This is one of the fundamental rules of accounting. The accounting equation can never be out of balance. Assets will always equal liabilities and owner's equity.

Expanded Accounting Equation

o What is the Expanded Accounting Equation?

The expanded accounting equation takes the basic accounting equation and splits equity into its four main elements: owner's capital, owner's withdrawals, revenues, and expenses. Both the assets and liabilities section of the basic equation remains the same in the expanded equation.

Expanding the equity section shows how equity created from two main sources: investors' contributions and company profits. Conversely, equity it decreased by investors leaving the company and company losses.

The expanded accounting equation also demonstrates the relationship between the balance sheet and the income statement by seeing how revenues and expenses flow through into the equity of the company.

Since corporations, partnerships, and sole proprietorships are different types of entities, they have different types of owners. For instance, corporations have stockholders and paid-in capital accounts; where as, partnerships have owner's contribution and distribution accounts. Thus, all of these entities have a slightly different expanded equation.

Accounts

o **What is an Account?**

Accounts are at the foundation of financial accounting. Each business transaction increases or decreases balances in one account or another. The entire accounting concept is based on maintaining a chart of accounts, but what is an account?

An account is simply a record of all changes to a specific asset, liability, or equity item. You can think of an account like a notepad. Each accounting item has its own notepad that is used to document all of the increases and decreases to that item over time.

For instance, the asset account records all of the changes in assets over time like asset purchases and sales.

Accounts are typically named and numbered in order to categorize and keep track of them. Accounts can also have sub-accounts. For example, the vehicle account is a sub-account inside the main asset account.

All accounts are kept or recorded in the general ledger. You could think of this as a folder that you keep all of your account notepads in.

o **Types of Accounts**

All accounting in the chart of accounts or general ledger fall into three main categories: asset, liability, or equity.

Asset accounts have a debit balance and represent the resources a company has at its disposal.

Liability accounts have a credit balance and represent the money that a company owes to other entities.

Equity accounts also have a credit balance and they represent the owners' stake in the company.

o **Account Format**

There are many different ways to format or display an account, but the most common way is by using T-accounts. T-accounts format account balances by keeping the debits on the left side and the credits on the right. The overall account balance is then calculated at the bottom. T-accounts also have a title or heading that displays the name and number of the account.

Here is an example of a T-account.

Sample T-Account	
Debits (left side)	Credits (right side)
Totals	Totals

Accounts can also be displayed as a listing of transactions in the general ledger. In other words, the cash account might just have a list of all the transactions that affected the cash account during that period.

Although the list format ultimately works, T-accounts and similar reports are much easier to read and use. T-accounts are also helpful in the accounting cycle before preparing trial balances.

Asset Accounts

o **What is an Asset Account? – Definition**

An asset is defined as a resource that is owned or controlled by a company that can be used to provide a future economic benefit. In other words, assets are items that a company uses to generate future revenues or maintain its operations.

Assets accounts generally have a debit balance. This means that entries created on the left side (debit entries) of an asset T-account increase the asset account balance while journal entries created on the right side (credit entries) decrease the account balance.

o **Types of Asset Accounts – Explanation**

Pretty much all accounting systems separate groups of assets into different accounts. These accounts are organized into current and non-current categories. A current asset is one that has a useful life of one year or less. Non-current assets have a useful life of longer than one year.

o **List of Assets Accounts – Examples**

Here's a list of some of the most common asset accounts fond in a chart of accounts:

Current Assets

Cash – Cash is the most liquid asset a company can own. It includes any form of currency that can be readily traded including coins, checks, money orders, and bank account balances.

Accounts Receivable – Accounts Receivable is an asset that arises from selling goods or services to someone on credit. The receivable is a promise from the buyer to pay the seller according to the terms of the sale. This is an unusual asset because it isn't an asset at all. It is more of a claim to an asset. The seller has a claim on the buyer's cash until the buyer pays for the goods or services.

Notes Receivable – A note is a written promise to repay money. A company that holds notes signed by another entity has an asset recorded as a note. Unlike accounts receivable, notes receivable can be long-term assets with a stated interest rate.

Prepaid Expenses – Prepaid expenses, like prepaid insurance, are expenses that have been paid in advanced. Like accounts receivable, prepaid expenses are assets because they are a claim to assets. If six months worth of insurance is paid in advance, the company is entitled to insurance (a service) for the next six months in the future.

Inventory – Inventory consists of goods owned a company that is in the business of selling those goods. For example, a car would be considered inventory for a car dealership because it is in the business of selling cars. A car would not be considered inventory for a pizza restaurant looking to selling it delivery car.

Supplies – Many companies have miscellaneous assets that are entire in product production that are too small and inexpensive to capitalize. These assets are expenses when they are purchased. A good example is car factory's bolts. It's difficult to account for each bolt as it is used in the assembly process, so they are just expensed.

Long-term Assets

Fixed Assets – Fixed assets include equipment, vehicles, machinery, and even computers. These assets generally have a useful life of more than one year and are usually more expensive business purchases.

Intangible Assets – Not all assets are physical. Some assets like goodwill, stock investments, patents, and websites can't be touched. These intellectual assets can be quite substantial, however.

Liability Accounts

o **What is a Liability Account? – Definition**

Liabilities are defined as debts owed to other companies. In a sense, a liability is a creditor's claim on a company' assets. In other words, the creditor has the right to confiscate assets from a company if the company doesn't pay it debts. Most state laws also allow creditors the ability to force debtors to sell assets in order to raise enough cash to pay off their debts.

Debt financing is often used to fund operations or expansions. These debts usually arise from business transactions like purchases of goods and services. For example, a business looking to purchase a building will usually take out a mortgage from a bank in order to afford the purchase. The business then owes the bank for the mortgage and contracted interest.

Liability accounts have a credit balance. This means that entries created on the left side (debit entries) of a liability T-account decrease the liability account balance while journal entries created on the right side (credit entries) increase the account balance.

o Types of Liability Accounts – Examples

There are many different kinds of liability accounts, although most accounting systems groups these accounts into two main categories: current and non-current. Current liabilities are debts that become due within the year, while non-current liabilities are debts that become due greater than one year in the future. Here are some examples of both current and non-current liabilities:

Current Liabilities

Accounts Payable – Many companies purchase inventory on credit from vendors or supplies. When the supplier delivers the inventory, the company usually has 30 days to pay for it. This obligation to pay is referred to as payments on account or accounts payable. No written contract needs to be in place. The promise to pay can be either oral or even implied.

Accrued Expenses – Since accounting periods rarely fall directly after an expense period, companies often incur expenses but don't pay them until the next period. These expenses are called accrued liabilities. Take utilities for example. The current month's utility bill is usually due the following month. Once the utilities are used, the company owes the utility company. These utility expenses are accrued and paid in the next period.

Non-current Liabilities

Bonds Payable – Many companies choose to issue bonds to the public in order to finance future growth. Bonds are essentially contracts to pay the bondholders the face amount plus interest on the maturity date. Bonds are usually long-term liabilities.

Notes Payable – A note payable is a long-term contract to borrow money from a creditor. The most common notes payable are mortgages and personal notes.

Unearned Revenue – Unearned revenue is slightly different from other liabilities because it doesn't involve direct borrowing. Unearned revenue arises when a company sells goods or services to a customer who pays the company but doesn't receive the goods or services. In effect, this customer paid in advance for is purchase. The company must recognize a liability because it owes the customer for the goods or services the customer paid for.

Equity Accounts

o **What is an Equity Account? – Definition**

Equity is defined as the owner's interest in the company assets. In other words, upon liquidation after all the liabilities are paid off, the shareholders own the remaining assets. This is why equity is often referred to as net assets or assets minus liabilities.

Equity can be created by either owner contributions or by the company retaining its profits. When an owner contributes more money into the business to fund its operations, equity in the company increases. Likewise, if the company produces net income for the year and doesn't distribute that money to its owner, equity increases.

Equity accounts, like liabilities accounts, have credit balances. This means that entries created on the left side (debit entries) of an equity T-account decrease the equity account balance while journal entries created on the right side (credit entries) increase the account balance.

o **Types of Equity Accounts – Explanation**

There are several types of equity accounts illustrated in the expanded accounting equation that all affect the overall equity balance differently. Here are the main types of equity accounts.

Capital – Capital consists of initial investments made by owners. Stock purchases or partnership buy-ins are considered capital because both are comprised of cash contributions made by the owners to the company. Capital accounts have a credit balance and increase the overall equity account.

Withdrawals – Owner withdrawals are the opposite of contributions. This is where the company distributes cash to its owners. Withdrawals have a debit balance and always reduce the equity account.

Revenues – Revenues are the monies received by a company or due to a company for providing goods and services. The most common examples of revenues are sales, commissions earned, and interest earned. Revenue has a credit balance and increases equity when it is earned.

Expenses – Expenses are essentially the costs incurred to produce revenue. Costs like payroll, utilities, and rent are necessary for business to operate. Expenses are contra equity accounts with debit balances and reduce equity.

o **Examples**

Unlike assets and liabilities, equity accounts vary depending on the type of entity. For example, partnerships and corporations use different equity accounts because they have different legal requirements to fulfil. Here are some examples of both sets of equity accounts.

Partnership Equity Accounts

Owner's or Member's Capital – The owner's capital account is used by partnerships and sole proprietors that consists of contributed capital, invested capital, and profits left in the business. This account has a credit balance and increases equity.

Owner's Distributions – Owner's distributions or owner's draw accounts show the amount of money the owners have taken out of the business. Distributions signify a reduction of company assets and company equity.

Corporate Equity Accounts

Common Stock – Common stock is an equity account that records the amount of money investors initially contributed to the corporation for their ownership in the company. This is usually recorded at the par value of the stock.

Paid-In Capital – Paid-in capital, also called paid-in capital in excess of par, is the excess dollar amount above par value that shareholders contribute to the company. For instance, if an investor paid $10 for a $5 par value stock, $5 would be recorded as common stock and $5 would be recorded as paid-in capital.

Treasury Stock – Sometimes corporations want to downsize or eliminate investors by purchasing company from shareholders. These shares that are purchased by the company are called treasury stock. This stock has a debit balance and reduces the equity of the company.

Dividends – Dividends are distributions of company profits to shareholders. Dividends are the corporate equivalent of partnership distributions. Both reduce the equity of the company.

Retained Earnings – Companies that make profits rarely distribute all of their profits to shareholders in the form of dividends. Most companies keep a significant share of their profits to reinvest and help run the company operations. Some profits that are kept within the company are called retained earnings.

Contra Account

○ What is a Contra Account? Definition

A contra account is an account with a balance opposite the normal accounts in its category. Contra accounts are usually linked to specific accounts on the balance sheet and are reported as subtractions from these accounts. In other words, contra accounts are used to reduce normal accounts on the balance sheet.

○ Types of Contra Accounts – Explanation

There are a few different types of contra accounts in the chart of accounts. Each one is tied to their respective asset, liability, or equity account to reduce their carrying balance on the balance sheet. Here's a list of the main types of contra accounts:

Contra Asset Account – A contra asset account is an asset that carries a credit balance and is used to decrease the balance of another asset on the balance. An example of this is accumulated depreciation. This account decreases the fixed asset carrying balance.

Contra Liability Account – A contra liability account is a liability that carries a debit balance and decreases other liabilities on the balance sheet. An example of this is a discount on bonds payable.

Contra Equity Account – A contra equity account has a debit balance and decreases a standard equity account. Treasure stock is a good example as it carries a debit balance and decreases the overall stockholders' equity.

o **Example**

How are Contra Accounts Used and Reported?

Take the equipment account for example. Equipment is a long-term asset account that has a debit balance. Equipment is depreciated over its useful. This depreciation is saved in a contra asset account called accumulated depreciation. The accumulated depreciation account has a credit balance and is used to reduce the carrying value of the equipment. The balance sheet would report equipment at its historical cost and then subtract the accumulated depreciation.

By reporting contra accounts on the balance sheet, users can learn even more information about the company than if the equipment was just reported at its net amount. Balance sheet readers cannot only see the actual cost of the item; they can also see how much of the asset was written off as well as estimate the remaining useful life and value of the asset.

The same is true for other asset accounts like accounts receivable. Accounts receivable is rarely reported on the balance sheet at its net amount. Instead, it is reported at its full amount with an allowance for bad debts listed below it. This shows investors how much receivables are still good. Maybe more importantly, it shows investors and creditors what percentage of receivables the company is writing off.

Revenue Accounts

o **What is a Revenue Account?**

Revenues are the assets earned by a company's operations and business activities. In other words, revenues include the cash or receivables received by a company for the sale of its goods or services.

The revenue account is an equity account with a credit balance. This means that a credit in the revenue T-account increases the account balance. As shown in the expanded accounting equation, revenues increase equity. Unlike other accounts, revenue accounts are rarely debited because revenues or income are usually only generated. Income is rarely taken away from a company.

The revenue account is only debited if goods are returned and sales are refunded. In this case, the recorded sale must be reversed because the original sale is cancelled.

o **Types of Revenue Accounts – Examples**

There are many different kinds of revenue accounts, but they all represent the same basic concepts: a company receives cash or a claim to cash for the sale or use of its assets. Revenues are typically separated into two different categories: operating revenues and non-operating revenues or other income.

Operating Revenues

Operating revenues are generated from a company's main business activities. In other words, this is the area of activities that a company earns most of its income and chooses to operate. Microsoft's operating revenue comes from software development and creation because it is a software company.

Here are some examples of operating revenues:

Sales – A sale is an exchange of goods for cash or a claim to cash. Sales are typically made by manufacturers, wholesalers, and retailers when they sell their inventory to customers. For example, a clothing retailer would record the income from selling a shirt to a customer as a sale or a merchandise sale

Rents – Rental income is earned by a landlord for allowing tenants to reside in his or her building or land. The tenants often have to sign a rental contract that dictates the details of the rental payments. According to the accrual method of accounting, the landlord records rental income when it is earned – not paid.

Consulting Services – Consulting service or professional services include all income from providing a service to a customer or client. For example, a law firm records professional service revenues when it provides legal services for a client.

Non-operating Revenues or Other Income

Other income includes all revenues generated by a company outside of its normal operations. Usually non-operating revenues are only a fraction of operating revenues.

Here is an example of non-operating revenues:

Interest income – Interest income is the most common form of non-operating income because most businesses earn small amounts of interest from their savings and checking accounts. Interest income is not only limited to bank account interest. It can also include interest earned from accounts receivable or other contracts.

Expense Account

○ **What is an Expense Account?**

Expenses are the costs incurred to generate revenues. In other words, a firm records an expense when it disburses cash or promises to disburse cash for an asset or service used to generate income. A manufacturer would record an expense when it pays its employees for producing its products.

Expenses accounts are equity accounts with a debit balance. Expense accounts are considered contra equity accounts because their balance decreases the overall equity balance. In other words, debiting an expense account increases the balance instead of decreasing it like most other equity accounts.

Expenses are subtracted from revenues to calculate overall equity in the expanded accounting equation and calculate net income on the income statement.

○ **Types of Expense Accounts – Examples**

There are tons of different expense accounts. Think about how many costs a business incurs to produce and sell a product. Everything from production costs to selling costs is included in the main expense account.

Just like revenues, expenses are generally separated into two main categories: operating and non-operating.

Operating Expenses

Operating expenses include all costs that are incurred to generate operating revenues like merchandise sales. Here are some examples of common operating expenses.

Rent – Businesses that can't afford to purchase a space to operate usually rent a space from another company. These monthly rental payments are recorded as an expense. Buildings and floor space aren't the only thing rented, however. Equipment and vehicles are also commonly rented by businesses.

Wages – Employers have to pay their employees to perform operations in the company. Some employees produce goods while others perform administrative functions like bookkeeping. The company pays all of these employees for their time and efforts. These payments are recorded as wages or salary expenses.

Utilities – Utilities costs include electricity, water, heat, and even telephone services. These payments are necessary any business to operate.

Advertising – Advertising consists of payments made to another company to promote products or services. Just about every company advertises their products or services in one way or another. These payments are recorded as operating expenses because they help sell generate operating revenues.

Non-operating Expenses

Non-operating expenses include costs that can't be linked back to operating revenues. Interest expense is the most common non-operating expense.

Interest Expense – Interest is the cost of borrowing cash for a period of time. Loans from banks or bonds usually require regular interest payments to compensate the lender. These payments don't generate operating income, so they are recorded as a non-operating expense.

General Ledger

o **What is the General Ledger?**

A general ledger or accounting ledger is a record or document that contains account summaries for accounts used by a company. In other words, a ledger is a record that details all business accounts and account activity during a period. Remember our notebook analogy in the account explanation? You can think of an account as a notebook filled with business transactions from a specific account, so the cash notebook would have records of all the business transactions involving cash.

By this same analogy, a ledger could be considered a folder that contains all of the notebooks or accounts in the chart of accounts. For instance, the ledger folder could have a cash notebook, accounts receivable notebook, and notes receivable notebooks in it. In a sense, a ledger is a record or summary of the account records.

A ledger is often referred to as the book of second entry because business events are first recorded in journals. After the journals are complete for the period, the account summaries are posted to the ledger.

o **List of General Ledger Accounts and Content**

Accounting Ledger

The general ledger is often called the accounting ledger because it contains a listing of all general accounts in the accounting system's chart of accounts. Here are the main types of general ledger accounts:

- Asset Accounts (Cash, Accounts Receivable, Fixed Assets)

- Liability Accounts (Accounts Payable, Bonds Payable, Long-Term Debt)

- Stockholders' Equity Accounts (Common Stock, Retained Earnings)

- Revenue Accounts (Sales, Fees)

- Expense Accounts (Wages Expense, Utilities Expense, Depreciation Expense)

- Other Gain and Loss Accounts (Interest Expense, Investment Income, Gain/Loss on Disposal of Asset)

These accounts are debited and credited to record transactions throughout the year. Most modern companies use a computerized GL, like the one in QuickBooks software packages, to track their business transactions. This way reports can be automatically generated and there

- **Example**

How to Use the General Ledger

Accounts are usually listed in the general ledger with their account numbers and transaction information. Here is what a general ledger template looks like in debit and credit format.

General Ledger			
Account Number	Account Description	Debits	Credits
1	Assets	100	
2	Liabilities		10
3	Equity		90
Totals		100	100

As you can see, columns are used for the account numbers, account titles, and debit or credit balances. The debit and credit format makes the ledger look similar to a trial balance. Other ledger formats list individual transaction details along with account balances.

Accounting ledgers can be displayed in many different ways, but the concept is still the same. Ledgers summarize the balances of the accounts in the chart of accounts.

- o **Subsidiary Ledgers**

The general ledger is not the only ledger in an accounting system. Subsidiary ledgers include selective accounts unlike the all-encompassing general ledger. Sometimes subsidiary ledgers are used as an intermediate step before posting journals to the general ledger.

For instance, cash activity is usually recorded in the cash receipts journal. The account details can then be posted to the cash subsidiary ledger for management to analyse before it is posted to the general ledger for reporting purposes.

Now let us move on to talk about debits vs. credits and how they work in an accounting system.

Debits and Credits

o **Debit vs Credit – What's the Difference?**

The double entry accounting system is based on the concept of debits and credits. This is an area where many new accounting students get confused. Often people think debits mean additions while credits mean subtractions. This isn't the case at all.

Debits and credits actually refer to the side of the ledger that journal entries are posted to. A debit, sometimes abbreviated as Dr., is an entry that is recorded on the left side of the accounting ledger or T-account. Conversely, a credit or Cr. is an entry on the right side of the ledger.

This right-side, left-side idea stems from the accounting equation where debits always have to equal credits in order to balance the mathematically equation.

Accounting Equation		
Debits =	Credits	+ Credits
Assets =	Liabilities + Equity	

If you will notice, debit accounts are always shown on the left side of the accounting equation while credit accounts are shown on the right side. Thus, debit entries are always recorded on the left and credit entries are always recorded on the right.

So debits and credits don't actually mean plusses and minuses. Instead, they reflect account balances and their relationship in the accounting equation.

o **Debit and Credit Accounts and Their Balances**

There are several different types of accounts in an accounting system. Each account is assigned either a debit balance or credit balance based on which side of the accounting equation it falls. Here are the main three types of accounts.

Assets

All normal asset accounts have a debit balance. This means that asset accounts with a positive balance are always reported on the left side of a T-Account. Assets are increased by debits and decreased by credits.

Liabilities

All normal liabilities have a credit balance. In other words, these accounts have a positive balance on the right side of a T-Account. Liabilities are increased by credits and decreased by debits.

Equity Accounts

Equity accounts like retained earnings and common stock also have a credit balances. This means that equity accounts are increased by credits and decreased by debits.

Contra Accounts

Notice I said that all "normal" accounts above behave that way. Well, what is an un-normal account? Contra accounts are accounts that have an opposite debit or credit balance. For instance, a contra asset account has a credit balance and a contra equity account has a debit balance. These accounts are used to reduce normal accounts. For example, accumulated depreciation is a contra asset account that reduces a fixed asset account.

o **Credit vs Debit Examples**

— Suellen Furniture Company needs to buy a new delivery truck because their current truck is started to fall apart. Suellen purchases the new truck for $5,000, so he writes a check to the car company and receives the truck in exchange. Suellen cash is being reduced by the $5,000 and his fixed assets are being increased by $5,000. Suellen would record this entry like this:

Example Journal Entry			
Date	Account Name	Debit	Credit
December 31			
	Vehicle	5,000.00	
	-Cash		5,000.00
	To record purchase of new vehicle.		

As you can see, Suellen's cash is credited (decreased) and his vehicles account is debited (increased).

— Now let us take the same example as above except let's assume Suellen paid for the truck by taking out a loan. Suellen's vehicle account would still increase by $5,000, but his cash would not decrease because he is paying with a loan. Instead, his liabilities account would increase.

Example Journal Entry			
Date	Account Name	Debit	Credit
December 31			
	Vehicle	5,000.00	
	-Vehicle Liability		5,000.00
	To record purchase of new vehicle on credit.		

As you can see, Suellen's liabilities account is credited (increased) and his vehicles account is debited (increased).

— Now let's assume that Suellen's Furniture didn't purchase the truck at all. It could not afford to buy a new one, so Suellen just contributed his personal truck to the company. In this case, Suellen's vehicle account would still increase, but his cash and liabilities would stay the same. Suellen's equity account would increase because he contributed the truck.

Example Journal Entry			
Date	Account Name	Debit	Credit
December 31			
	Vehicle	5,000.00	
	-Equity (Owner's Contribution)		5,000.00
	To record owner's contribution of vehicle.		

As you can see, Suellen's equity account is credited (increased) and his vehicles account is debited (increased).

Double Entry Accounting

o What is Double-Entry Accounting?

Double entry accounting, also called double entry bookkeeping, is the accounting system that requires every business transaction or event to be recorded in at least two accounts. This is the same concept behind the accounting equation. Every debit that is recorded must be matched with a credit. In other words, debits and credits must also be equal in every accounting transaction and in their total.

Every modern accounting system is built on the double entry bookkeeping concept because every business transaction affects at least two different accounts. For example, when a company takes out a loan from a bank, it receives cash from the loan and also creates a liability that it must repay in the future. This single transaction affects both the asset accounts and the liabilities accounts.

o Example

How to Use Double Entry Accounting

Let's take a look at the accounting equation to illustrate the double entry system. Here is the equation with examples of how debits and credit affect all of the accounts.

Accounting

Accounting Equation								
Assets		=	Liabilities		+	Equity		
Debits	Credits		Debits	Credits		Debits	Credits	
⬆	⬇		⬇	⬆		⬇	⬆	
Increase	Decrease		Decrease	Increase		Decrease	Increase	

As you can see from the equation, assets always have to equal liabilities plus equity. In other words, overall debits must always equal overall credits. For example, if an asset account is increased or debited, either a liability or equity account must be increased or credited for the same amount.

This is always the case except for when a business transaction only affects one side of the accounting equation. For example, if a restaurant purchases a new delivery vehicle for cash, the cash account is decreased by the cash disbursement and increased by the receipt of the new vehicle. This transaction does not affect the liability or equity accounts, but it does affect two different assets accounts. Thus, assets are decreased and immediately increased resulting in a net effect of zero.

The concept of double entry accounting is the basis for recording business transaction and journal entries. Make sure you have a good understanding of this concept before moving on past the accounting basics section.

Now that we have talked about the double entry bookkeeping system, let's move on to recording journal entries.

Business Events

o **What is a Business Event?**

A Business event, also called a business transaction, is an exchange of value between two different groups. The exchange is usually called an event when it impacts the accounting equation in one way or another. In other words, a business transaction or event occurs when the assets, liabilities, or owner's equity of a company is changed.

We are all familiar with transaction. For example, when you purchase groceries, you give the cashier money and you leave with a bag of groceries. Business transactions work the same way.

An event always impacts the accounting equation of a company because it is an exchange of financial statement elements for other financial statement elements.

o Journal Entry Format

All accounting events are recorded in a company's accounting system as journal entries as they occur. These journal entries simply record the changes to the accounting equation based on the business transaction. Taking our grocery example above, a journal entry would be recorded to decrease the cash account by the amount paid to the cashier and increase the supplies account by the same amount.

Journal Entry Format			
Date	Account Name	Debit	Credit
January 1			
	Debited Account	xxxx	
	-Credited Account		xxxx
	Description of the Journal Entry		

The journal entry system is based on debits and credits to increase or decrease account balances. Every journal entry's debits and credits must balance. This is the same concept behind the accounting equation. For every dollar debited to one account in an entry, the same amount must be credited to a different account. This way the accounting equation is always in balance.

o **Example**

How are Business Events Recorded?

Here is an example of the journal entry format for our grocery purchase transaction.

Journal Entry Format			
Date	Account Name	Debit	Credit
January 1			
	Supplies	100.00	
	-Cash		100.00
	Purchase company supplies		

As you can see, the supplies account is debited or increased by the event while the cash account is credited or decreased by the event. A standard journal entry always shows the date of business transaction, names of the accounts effected, amounts to be debited and credited, as well as a brief description of the event.

When you are first learning how to make journal entries it is helpful to look at how these entries affect the accounting equation. Here's a look at the same transaction's effect on the accounting equation.

Accounting Equation				
$100	$100			
⬇	⬆			
Assets	=	Liabilities	+	Equity

As you can see, both accounts in the journal entry are asset accounts. Thus, total assets are increased from newly purchases supplies and decreased by the disbursement of cash. In other words, there is no net change to the equation. However, notice that the equation is still in balance after the transaction is made.

General Journal

o **What is a General Journal?**

The general journal, also called the book of first entry, is a record of business transactions and events for a specific account. In other words, this journal chronologically stores all the journal entries for a specific account or group of account in one place, so management and bookkeepers can analyse the data.

Accounting journals are often called the book of first entry because this is where journal entries are made. Once a business transaction is made, the bookkeeper records that event in the form of a journal entry in one of the accounting journals. Then, at the end of a period, the journals are posted to accounting ledgers for reporting purposes.

Companies use many different journals depending on their accounting system and industry, but all companies use the general journal.

o **General Journal Contents**

The general journal is an accounting journal used to record journal entries for all types of transactions. Many companies use this journal exclusively to record all of their journal entries in the entire accounting system. There are pros and cons to this approach as it tends to make the journal extremely large and is difficult to search. Even the smallest businesses' GL would be 200-500 pages.

Having something this large typically isn't practical, so most companies use the GL only to record general items like depreciation. Transactions that can fit into a more specific categories can be recorded in special accounting journals. We'll talk more about these in a bit.

You can think of it like this. The General Journal is a catch-all journal where transactions that don't fit into special categories are recorded. All modern GLs are computerized with accounting software, so GL maintenance is pretty simple. Now that we know what is in the GL, let's take a look at how it is formatted.

o **Format and Template**

Most journals are formatted the same way with columns for the transaction dates, account names, debit and credit amounts, as well as a brief description of the transaction. Does this sound familiar? It should. This is a typical journal entry format. That's all a journal is. It's just a list of journal entries recorded in one place.

Here's a general journal template example.

Journal Entry Format			
Date	Account Name	Debit	Credit
January 1			
	Debited Account	xxxx	
	-Credited Account		xxxx
	Description of the Journal Entry		

o **Example**

<u>**How to Use the General Journal**</u>

Throughout the accounting period, a business enters into transactions with customers, vendors, suppliers, the government, and other entities. All of these transactions must be recorded in order to accurately show the financial standings of the company at the end of the period.

In order to do this, a bookkeeper makes journal entries in the general journal recording changes in the corresponding accounts for a given transaction. For example, if a business purchased a new company vehicle for cash, the bookkeeper would record a journal entry that debits the vehicle account and credits the cash account.

At the end of the period, all of the entries in the general journal are tallied up in their corresponding accounts and are reported on the trial balance.

o **Special Journals**

Accounting Journals

In addition to the general journal, there are several special journals or subsidiary journals that are used to help divide and organize business transactions.

Here's a list of the special accounting journals used:

- Cash Receipts Journal
- Cash Disbursements Journal
- Purchases Journal
- Sales Journal
- Purchase Return Journal
- Sales Return Journal
- General Journal

Each of these journals has a special purpose and are used to record specific types of transactions. For example, the cash receipts journal contains all of the cash sale transactions. The accounts receivable or credit sales journal contains all the transactions for credit sales.

Other journals like the sales journal and cash disbursements journal are also used the help management organize and analyse accounting information.

Now that you understand the GL and how it's used, let's look at how to create a trial balance.

Trial Balance

o What is a Trial Balance?

A trial balance sheet is a report that lists the ending balances of each account in the chart of accounts in balance sheet order. Bookkeepers and accountants use this report to consolidate all of the T-accounts into one document and double check that all transactions were recorded in proper journal entry format.

Bookkeepers typically scan the year-end trial balance for posting errors to ensure that the proper accounts were debited and credited while posting journal entries. Internal accountants, on the other hand, tend to look at global trends of each account. For instance, they might notice that accounts receivable increased drastically over the year and look into the details to see why.

Tax accountants and auditors also use this report to prepare tax returns and begin the audit process. The TB format lends itself to a wide variety of uses.

o **Trial Balance Format**

The trial balance format is easy to read because of its clean layout. It typically has four columns with the following descriptions: account number, name, debit balance, and credit balance. It's always sorted by account number, so anyone can easily scan down the report to find an account balance. This order also tends to be in balance sheet order since the average chart of accounts follows the accounting equation starting with the assets.

Not all accounts in the chart of accounts are included on the TB, however. Usually only active accounts with year-end balance are included in the TB because accounts with zero balances don't make it on the financial statements. For example, if a company had a vehicle at the beginning of the year and sold it before year-end, the vehicle account would not show up on the year-end report because it's not an active account.

The report also totals the debit and credit columns at the bottom. As with all financial accounting, the debits must equal the credits. If it's out of balance, something is wrong and the bookkeeper must go through each account to see what got posted or recorded incorrectly.

This step saves a lot time for accountants during the financial statement preparation process because they don't have to worry about the balance sheet and income statement being off due to an out-of-balance error. Keep in mind, this does not ensure that all journal entries were recorded accurately. It just means that the credits and debits balance.

A journal entry error can still exist. For instance, in our vehicle sale example the bookkeeper could have accidentally debited accounts receivable instead of cash when the vehicle was sold. The debits would still equal the credits, but the individual accounts are incorrect. This type of error can only be found by going through the trial balance sheet account by account.

Since most companies have computerized accounting systems, they rarely manually create a TB or have to check for out-of-balance errors. They computer system does that automatically.

o **Preparation and Process**

How is the Trial Balance Prepared?

When the accounting system creates the initial report, it is considered an unadjusted trial balance because no adjustments have been made to the chart of accounts. This is simply a list of all the account balances straight out of the accounting system.

As the bookkeepers and accountants examine the report and find errors in the accounts, they record adjusting journal entries to correct them. After these errors are corrected, the TB is considered an adjusted trial balance.

We still aren't done with this report yet though. The errors have been identified and corrected, but the closing entries still need to be made before this TB can used to create the financial statements. After the closing entries have been made to close the temporary accounts, the report is called the post-closing trial balance.

Let's take a look at an example.

o **Example**

How to use the Trial Balance

Here's an example trial balance. As you can see, the report has a heading that identifies the company, report name, and date that it was created. The accounts are listed on the left with the balances under the debit and credit columns.

Paul's Guitar Shop, Inc. Unadjusted Trial Balance December 31, 2015		
Account	**Debit**	**Credit**
Cash	$ 32,800	
Accounts Receivable	300	
Inventory	39,800	
Leasehold Improvements	100,000	
Accounts Payable		$ 49,000
Long-term Liabilities		99,500
Common Stock		10,000
Dividends	1,000	
Revenues		27,800
Cost of Goods Sold	10,200	
Rent Expense	500	
Supplies Expense	500	
Utilities Expense	200	
Wages Expense	500	
Interest Expense	500	
Totals	$ 186,300	$ (186,300)

Since the debit and credit columns equal each other totalling a zero balance, we can move in the year-end financial statement preparation process and finish the accounting cycle for the period.

Chart of Accounts

o What is the Chart of Accounts? – Definition

The chart of accounts is a list of every account in the general ledger of an accounting system. Unlike a trial balance that only lists accounts that are active or have balances at the end of the period, the chart lists all of the accounts in the system. It's a simple list of account numbers and names. It doesn't include any other information about each account like balances, debits, and credits like a trial balance does.

You can think of this like a rolodex of accounts that the bookkeeper and the accounting software can use to record transactions, make reports, and prepare financial statements throughout the year.

o Chart of Accounts Format and Number System

Each account is typically assigned a number based on the order it appears on the financial statements. Balance sheet accounts are usually presented first followed by income statement accounts. Thus, accounts are assigned numbers and listed in this order: assets, liabilities, equity, income, expenses, other.

Most companies use a numbering system that groups accounts into financial statement categories. For example, all asset accounts might have a prefix of 1 while liability accounts might have a prefix of 2. This numbering system looks like this:

- Assets: 1-001

- Liabilities: 2-001

- Equity: 3-001

- Revenues: 4-001

- Expenses: 5-001

- Other: 6-001

This numbering system helps bookkeepers and accountants keep track of accounts along with what category they belong two. For instance, if an account's name or description is ambiguous, the bookkeeper can simply look at the prefix to know exactly what it is. Take insurance for example. An account might simply be named "insurance offset." What does that mean? Is it a prepaid asset or an expense that was paid out? The bookkeeper would be able to tell the difference by the account number. An asset would have the prefix of 1 and an expense would have a prefix of 5. This structure can avoid confusion in the bookkeeper process and ensure the proper account is selected when recording transactions.

Tilly Maureens

Although most accounting software packages like QuickBooks come with a standard or default list of accounts, bookkeepers can set up and customize their account structure to fit their business and industry.

For example, many companies have different departments that incur similar costs like supplies. Management might want to evaluate the supplies expenses for each department to see which one is using its resources the most efficiently. To make this comparison easier, the bookkeeper could tag the expenses to different departments of simply use different numbered accounts for each department. Department 1 could use 5-001-1 for its supplies expense while department 2 could use 5-0001-2 to differentiate it from the other departments.

o **Example and Template**

How to Use the Chart of Accounts

There are many different ways to structure a chart of accounts, but the important thing to remember is that simplicity is key. The more accounts are added to the chart and the more complex the numbering system is, the more difficult it will be to keep track of them and actually use the accounting system. Simple is always better than complicated.

Here's a standard example chart of accounts.

Accounting

	Chart of Accounts		
Number	**Description**	**Account Type**	**Financial Statement**
1-001	Cash	Asset	Balance Sheet
1-010	Accounts Receivable	Asset	Balance Sheet
1-020	Prepaid Expenses	Asset	Balance Sheet
1-030	Inventory	Asset	Balance Sheet
1-040	Fixed Assets	Asset	Balance Sheet
1-050	Accumulated Depreciation	Asset	Balance Sheet
1-060	Other Assets	Asset	Balance Sheet
2-001	Accounts Payable	Liability	Balance Sheet
2-010	Accrued Liabilities	Liability	Balance Sheet
2-020	Taxes Payable	Liability	Balance Sheet
2-030	Payroll Payable	Liability	Balance Sheet
2-040	Notes Payable	Liability	Balance Sheet
3-001	Common Stock	Equity	Balance Sheet
3-010	Retained Earnings	Equity	Balance Sheet
3-020	Additional Paid in Capital	Equity	Balance Sheet
4-001	Revenue	Revenue	Income Statement
4-010	Sales returns and allowances	Revenue	Income Statement
5-001	Cost of Goods Sold	Expense	Income Statement
5-010	Advertising Expense	Expense	Income Statement
5-020	Bank Fees	Expense	Income Statement
5-030	Depreciation Expense	Expense	Income Statement
5-040	Payroll Tax Expense	Expense	Income Statement
5-050	Rent Expense	Expense	Income Statement
5-060	Supplies Expense	Expense	Income Statement
5-070	Utilities Expense	Expense	Income Statement
5-080	Wages Expense	Expense	Income Statement
6-001	Other Expenses	Other	Income Statement

As you can see, each account is listed numerically in financial statement order with the number in the first column and the name or description in the second column.

o **How to Create a Chart of Accounts**

There are a few things that you should keep in mind when you are building a chart of accounts for your business.

Numbering – Don't use all concurrent numbers for your accounts. You will probably need to add accounts in the future. If you don't leave gaps in between each number, you won't be able to add new accounts in the right order. For example, assume your cash account is 1-001 and your accounts receivable account is 1-002, now you want to add a petty cash account. Well, this should be listed between the cash and accounts receivable in the chart, but there isn't a number in between them. Look at the number pattern in our example above.

Size – Set up your chart to have enough accounts to record transactions properly, but don't go over board. The more accounts you have, the more difficult it will be consolidate them into financial statements and reports. Also, it's important to periodically look through the chart and consolidate duplicate accounts.

Changes – It's inevitable that you will need to add accounts to your chart in the future, but don't drastically change the numbering structure and total number of accounts in the future. A big change will make it difficult to compare accounting record between these years.

<u>Conclusion</u>

You should now have a clearer idea of the context in which accounting is set. You should also be aware that accounting is the recording and processing of data into information, of the characteristics of 'good' information, and of the relationship between accounting and organisational objectives. This Book has introduced some of the basics of accounting.